SOMETIMES WE WALK
WITH OUR NAILS OUT

SOMETIMES WE WALK WITH OUR NAILS OUT

SARAH BARTLETT

SUBITO PRESS 2016

ISBN: 978-0-9906612-3-8

Design & typesetting by HR Hegnauer | www.hrhegnauer.com
Text typeset in Adobe Garamond Pro
Cover Design by Sara Van Dyke

Subito Press
Department of English
University of Colorado at Boulder
226 UCB
Boulder, CO 80309-0226
subitopress.org

Distributed by Small Press Distribution
1341 Seventh Street
Berkeley, California 94710
spdbooks.org

Generous funding for this publication has been provided by the Creative
Writing Program in the Department of English and the Innovative Seed
Grant Program at the University of Colorado at Boulder.

I. Freud Blah Blah Blah

II. De Animation

III. The Other Transcendence

Awakening is a parachute jump from the dream.
Tomas Tranströmer

The self forms at the edge of desire,
and a science of self arises
in effort to leave that self behind.
Anne Carson

I.
FREUD BLAH BLAH BLAH

When you take apart the small thing there is
always a perfect, blue egg on the inside.
Once I found one on the ground unbroken
and took it home to hatch. Little incubator,
little devil swathed in a child's chest.

Wood has its own animal smell: hot honey,
snails and sap dripping. What a thing
for thighs to hold on to. Leaves are not a joke
but that kind of magic grows on trees.
Branches claw every background
they're set against. I drape around the trunk
and let veins twist tight inside me.

We go to a rock show and touch shoulders.
I mark this in my mental calendar
with a star. We keep leaning in.
The band has faux celestial events
as a backdrop for their folk jams.
Pine trees keep everything
rooted in the present. Act Like
You've Been Swallowed By A Whale,
the lead singer instructs, so we do.

Be quiet and point to where your heart is—
this is not a useless exercise. I see you
in CMYK but I want to be overcome by M.
Saturation is a tipping point. It's almost imaginary
when it's all by itself, like the color you see
behind your eyes when you get hit in the face.

Inside the sweat machine we run our mouths
around until our teeth mean something different.
My body wants to meet your body in a dark alley
and say things in Braille. When I leave notes
on your pillow it's supposed to be a gimmick. Still,
here we are in love, careening toward death like a flower.

I'll make you a wolverine fur coat so you can climb
mountains and get your picture taken by
someone in a helicopter while waving a flag
that says Truth & Love. Staked at the top,
you'll feel the earth take a breath before it shakes
you loose. This is the kind of romance
I'm capable of right now.

I will Evel Knievel you so hard until fish come out
your eyes the same color as bar fights.
Your tight pants aren't tight enough for me.
Let's put tighter pants on. Let's press our pants
together and pray the blind gods on the surface
stop trying to pull us up to where the air is.

Where the supplies come from is immaterial—
there are always enough. Memory has
its own agenda: the white spark of skin,
crinkle of saliva decorating our bodies
like paint. Mary Shelley would understand
these approximations. I'm getting close as
a diary to the spot where you crouch, ashamed,
like some kind of miracle.

Last night I dreamt you were a Cat Stevens record
that skips on Moonshadow. I wake up and fall in love
with this flaw specifically. I call you and hang up
even though you say 'I know it's you.' I spend
all evening baking you cornbread. The last thing
in the world I want is for you to be hungry.

I sit in the swing and begin my trajectory.
What kind of person doesn't crave an uptick,
the ground parenthetical? You push hard
from behind. I rise until my head is the trees.
The park cracks open and we tumble out wet,
hurry home to lay each other carefully across
the sheets. This catapult a light-like interval
before the Moon starts wailing.

Your purple t-shirt should have a horse on it—
your chest would be under the horse's chest.

Can I live vicariously through your ekphrasis?
Art is an arm but a shitty hugger. Its shadow can be
pinned down and put on a wall. Paris wants you
to like it better than London—they are both full
of graves. Vestigial marble bodies people buildings
the size of stadiums and you are lost inside.

The shape your head leaves on the pillow
is a black cat. I choke on it, fur lining my throat.
I write out the coordinates for every secret
and leave them in your drawer. We all hold
a promise and a lie between our legs. An installation
of arrivals, stark and sudden as a blank wall
where something used to be hanging.

The holes in our rhetoric are showing—
nighttime wraps around a storm's arrival
and begins to shake. My father taught me to punch
with my thumb outside my fist, how to outrun a bear.
Survival depends on a number of duplicities.
I make recordings of sirens wailing
and play them loudly during arguments.
We wake up no matter what, greedier
than crows in the morning.

When we go into the jungle, I'm tired of being the one
who wears the grenades. My hands are grenades.
My teeth. My breasts. This turns us both on,
but contact is not advisable as such. You write me
into ransom notes, our enemy's greatest threat.
When we take them off at night, I don't know how
to be alone. Even the trees lean away.

Pets are stupid. I've never understood why
we want to clean up another animal's shit.
We already live inside of one that constantly
needs to be fed and cleaned and put down
for naps. My hand likes to be held.
I keep telling you.

I want to drop a tiny white feather into you.
I want to discover at the last second that
I'm a witch doctor and pull indecision out
like a wishbone. Waiting rooms are instructive,
but not that instructive.

Suffering is having your body full of nails.

Just replace your blood with nails and see what I mean.

What a mirror. What a black lake full of stars.

I paint a wall in my bedroom blue.
The mirror in the middle stores reflections
and plays them back: you walk in
and out. Undress. Arrange yourself next
to me. I buy a fish in a glass bubble
to authenticate the experience.
You go still, drifting on the surface.
I spend hours in front of the mirror,
keeping you afloat. The fish jumps out
of its bowl, shrinks like a popped balloon.
Hidden behind our building, the moon performs
its usual routine, disappointing no one.

My mother dreamt she gave birth to a wolf,
but I came out instead. My family jokes about this
over meals. Somewhere in the mountains a howl
is gathering. Somewhere guts spill across snow
like hot snakes—I try to explain over and over that
the pattern is remarkable for its beauty but they don't listen.
Stop signing your name every fucking place, they say,
and really mean it this time.

The buzz of the power lines is didactic:
I want to hold your project, its splintered pieces
gather the day deep into the sidewalk
and hold it there. Every question is a personal
question but that never stops me.
Once, I saw a dog run between the wheels
of a car and come out the other side missing
its tail. When I think about what I've lost,
nothing happens anymore.

II.
DE ANIMATION

All The Little Lights Turn On

I wake up with a forest growing
on my back, and instead of being alarmed,
I open my window and lay very still
so birds will move in.
My friends are concerned,
but I tell them not to touch it.
They sweep up fallen leaves
and bring me high-energy snacks.
They worry about how fast
it's taking over, whether or not
they should try and move me
before the room becomes overgrown,
and about the fox tail disappearing
into thickets. Paws make me feel
like I'm holding something.
They start sleeping over in tents.
Your body is going to be a killing field,
they warn. But I don't care
about hypocrisy anymore.

St. Augustine's Lost Entry

I look up how to spell "moustache"
and then look at fake moustaches online.
As I age my desires start to feel less unusual.
I dream I am mobbed by the desert—
I lay so still rattlesnakes sleep on my chest.
I wake, feel emptier. I levitate in the shower.
Crows are making death cries, so I check
the trunk of my car before I go anywhere
in case I'm being framed.
The heat is intransigent, scrapes my face
with its chin. Summer, you Goose.
I've got your eggs in my pocket
and I promise not to break them.

Swift In The Darkness

We press into the bar,
flowers in a bible.
A sock monkey sips
a glass of whiskey
at the next table.
I ask you if it's real
or if I'm asleep.
You have to tell me
to stop staring.
I draw you my best
cupid's bow in the restroom
with a piece of chalk,
voices lifting up my skirt.
Behind every door
another world attaches
a piece to the puzzle.

If I Could Only Find You, I'd Find You

I think about bullfighting in the shower
and drink whiskey and feel
how far away from myself
I've become. Power lines
in the middle of nowhere—
long, flat landscape that's there
for driving through and for coyotes.
I am keeping the crows away.
I can stand so still.
Somewhere else bullfighters
are making love to beautiful women;
they are sharp and fast
and in a hurry.
Their symphonic thighs twitch
in sleep, ready to make an escape.
The bull is quiet in its pen,
breathing into hay.
I have a million apologies
to hand out for other people.
I stay in the shower.
I steam up the windows
and make baby feet on the glass
with the outside of my hand.

There Was A Chance Of No Arrival

I walk to the store and buy
the smallest objects.
I take them with me on the airplane
where death hovers beneath me
and I ride it back to where I come from.
The storm throws light,
clouds are Simon,
and something keeps hitting
the yellow button until the battery
runs out and the music stops.
Off the plane, my objects
greet me at baggage claim.
My disappointment has wheels
for easy transport. I get tired
of the gods pretending to be us
pretending to be gods
who follow me home
so I won't be lonely.

Frontwards/Backwards

It's crowded at the party—
in the back room, people are
doing coke. It's almost cute,
except the dancing.
Someone has already produced
your first-born child
and there's a sadness
in the cold, hard fact of it.
I am a corporeal figurine.
You look like a ghost
under these lights, you say,
and position me
under your brightest arm.

Immortality Is So Whimsical

Swamps cradle their frogs
through the winter;
they don't feel time
passing the same way
we do. But they feel
the cold. I wish my arms
were bigger. Heaven
as a concept appeals,
but where do we go?
My body hates to think of it.
The aging lesbian with
purple hair watches me
walk to the bathroom
at the coffee shop.
I imagine her imagining
me with my pants down
and rush the experience.
We are all staving it off—
death, I mean. But still,
if six people have killed
themselves in your basement,
just don't let anyone else
into your basement.
We are bringing trees
inside the building
to make it plural.

New Faith

Love makes me gross.
The world expresses hopefulness
in the form of birdsong
and celestial necromancy and options.
This is a familiar itemization.
All the books won't save me—
I wake up in the morning
unsure of the last thing
I purchased. I forget myself
and try to remember.
I want to be your valentine,
just give me something
to believe in first.

Our Nuclear Payload Is Fully Loaded

I murdered your landscape—
I'm sorry.
My day leads me around
on a leash.
All this vegetation
was asking for it anyway,
angrier than a woman.
I love the world
so much
I can't stand it
anymore.
Red button
so Rudolph-y.
Let's make no
promises,
let's make dinner
and then push it.
The last moment
lasts forever.

Face Down In A Pool of Tears

Sometimes eyes make a sound
like a mousetrap. I sit around
and try to catch myself
in the machine, which is more than
a window and less than outside.
I'm hiding the machine from
the mice. Their delicate pink ears—
I can't stand it.

Wintertime Makes Me Honest

I haven't forgotten snow on the tongue—
tell me where to find the ad you are in.
I want your commerce on me—
it feels good to be dirty on Sunday.
The icicles don't stand a chance
but that doesn't stop me from
going tree to tree with my fingers bare.
Call the burn hotline: didn't they tell you
the whole world has gone missing
inside a single white envelope.

Sunday Is A Series Of Hands

When bags of leaves are tossed
off the roof, they hit the ground
like bodies—the clouds have
taken over their monotonous haul.
Your telescope is a metaphor,
but you can't use it here.
Don't you feel it?
Every broken thing just arrived
completely healed for the day.
In this diorama, you are the tree
and I am the same tree.
We are making a stand.
Miracles are rarely solvent.
Every day a woman
inside the darkest shrine
rubs sacred dirt on her
sorest parts, gets up to leave.
The sound she creates
while praying makes a mouse
jealous. It starts to eat
through the wall.

Camping

It is raining so hard
I think you are crumpling paper
in your sleep.
The van holds us still—
it is black as a hearse
with an opposite job.
You hold your son
so tightly you must dream
the same thing.
I dream of seeing a deer
running across a field.
I am the only one who sees it
and now there are
two of us.

Strange Bravery I Pay The Gods For

We close our eyes
so we don't have to see
each other. I drive my car
this way and die three times
a week. I keep coming back—
life is relentless in its lesson.
I drive my car past your house
with my eyes closed and arrive in
Atlantic City. I play the penny slots
and stare at Cleopatra.
I drop coins in her asp
and never get them back.
You drive past my house
with your eyes closed and hit
a crow standing in the street
eating fries from the day before.
You keep your eyes closed
and cry and die again
and wake up in your bed.
"Life is a series of accidents,"
you write in a letter to your father.
He still doesn't forgive you.

They Are Breathing All Around

1.

There are thousands of hummingbirds.
I watch them for hours in the morning.
They have replaced snow on the mountains.
Their throats are fuses.
They fire from their cannons.

2.

The mountains release all the animals.
Like doves at a wedding.
You sit listening to them in the dark.
Love they are right next to you.
They are breathing all around.

3.

Trees rise up and move toward the ridge.
Stands of elk are what is left behind.
They are almost invisible but we see them.
We move quietly into their midst.
Sharpen our beautiful antlers against every rock.

4.

We lay our bodies out in front of the fire.
You wrestle me into the right shape.
Kindling breaks and settles into burning.
There is only one true purpose.
I am the softest emptiest animal in your hands.

5.

A thunderstorm keeps arriving.
Orange cream puff clouds stack to infinity.
The mountains bite down.
We are right at the center of the maw.
We are where the tongue goes down.

6.

We climb the side of a mountain to a pond.
The pond's eye is closing.
We climb down the mountain.
The aspen leaves make their rattle.
This is a place where I am not a tourist.

7.

Between us and stars is hardly any air.
We take what's left for ourselves.
Beauty strings our eyes up.
It ties them to the door knob.
We tough it out under the blanket.

8.

A shadow of a bear streams behind the real bear.
I confuse the two.
The dark fur and its replication.
Somewhere ahead rocks frenzy falling water.
We rise up and rise up and rise up.

9.

My childhood map unrolls for you.
We go to the other side to explore.
We are in a hurry to get there before dark.
The big horn sheep ascend on silent elevators.
From the depths they appear just for us.

10.

Beads from your iced coffee on the varnish.
We let them spread into puddles.
The cabin fractures in morning light.
I crack eggs in the pan for breakfast.
This is where I always want to be standing.

Being Unhorsed Vs. Being Unsaddled

If only it would snow
and there were time to catalog
everything that stayed the same.
The farmer trucks out bails of hay
and everyday you are not
wild. Everyday you are
a circle of ice. Everyday
an absence louder than
the pounding of hooves.
The ground shakes with it;
you are not imagining
the metamorphosis.
Your body a deliverance,
a discard pile, an outreach
program, separation science.
You want to hear someone
say "that's the one I want."
You are standing by yourself.
Every morning you are on
the opposite side of the fence.
You don't know how it happened,
you just know it's happening.
There is a white horse
somewhere without you
or you are the white horse
somewhere with nothing to carry.

III.
THE OTHER TRANSCENDENCE

Being From Here

Are we really afraid
of the dog buried
under the shed
reaching out its bones
for a touch
Being alone isn't a final gesture
What I really want
is the resurrection of everyone
I ever loved
I will put them in a room
and never go inside
Death the eternal flapping veil
what we've been given
instead of wings
Names don't matter
it's a palpable thing
running between trees
memorizing the way we scream
The beautiful crux of it
unwraps light in the morning
and scatters the scraps
Eyes are explosives
their coned miracles so finite
you can feel them dimming
in front of the mirror
I am a reflection of you
being a reflection of her
being a reflection of her father
being a reflection of you

Journey

Why does it take so long
to get home
Half arrivals into hours
a doorway we keep entering
and entering and leaving
and entering until the day
wears itself out
Our veins a recycling heap
for the right words
you can't just say
I love you
you have to try harder
We are aware of this
We are almost there
We are riding fast in the cold
our words developing blindness
to a future without them
traveling behind
the whitest most beautiful
tail we've ever seen

The Hallelujah Chorus

I want to tell you
about the rattle of chains
under my school bus
So many histories collecting
a separate will
None of our entrances a door
We are all here
and each day we move
further into the ground
fields sprawling luscious
This is why I build on paper
where nothing is real

Auto-Autumnal

I can really feel my life
when the season
lifts its finger
off the bullet hole
Children dance like maniacs
through brittle piles
I am hopelessly optimistic
or the opposite is true
Cerise everywhere
spreading from
the branches
until we are all covered
On days like this
I am lonely
but not for you

A Mile Or A Million

This distance
a suction cup
outcast on the radio
I worry about my body
it's the one thing
that belongs to me
We arrive together
in ancient cities
and take notes on the smell
of stonework and blood
We are eager to catch up
despite our escape
into fresh arms
How humiliating
to remember all the others
touching themselves
in their natural beds

Free House

The red neck
of a horse holds up
the wall where nothing
is growing
We are alive here
baking bread
in our mouths
Your shirt keeps becoming
my shirt and overnight
we are in love
The bread makes it hard
to talk so we sign
how strange it feels
to never be hungry
We rest our stomachs
against each other
ribs interlaced
and our bodies finish
the application

We Are Both Right About Stars

We are hearts
aren't we pounding
feet on a bridge
Swifts flight patterns
move in sonatas on beat
Trees never say growing
is not a vocation
or demand

Take me
behind that rock
and redistribute
handfuls of golden hair
I am not afraid
of cold water
Fish flip like coins
they always land
heads up
What luck
the sun sinks
to hide in red

We are both right
about stars
because no one
is right about stars
I want to see you

when I wake up scared
Right in front of me
a thousand exaltations

Beginning the day
is unforgettable
let's promise something
Animals were here
before and after
The future counts
on us for a kind
of heralded arrival

You took photos
of me naked
being afraid of death's
pointless gesture
notwithstanding
The bluest water is
elusive on film
We use our eyes instead
We use our mouths

Branches dangle
feathers their crucible
Celebration
a daily object
hotter than the bank
Don't walk back to me

I'm saving your place
everywhere I go
without you
just in case

Sometimes We Walk With Our Nails Out

The temporary splice
of departure feels luxurious

I imagine you holding a tree up
while the rain populates your face

We practice keeping our distances intact

I squish like a wet blanket at the thought
of you coming back towards me
and begin to pick flowers

* * *

There are myriad of excuses
but none of them stick

I sit around thinking
of what's inside your pocket
We're no longer strangers

I am capable of so much cruelty
in the name of love

Aren't you

I find a field and put your hands in it
You never find the field
but your hands are burning

Harvest, the cleaver

We answer the days in monotone
until they answer back

I receive so much beauty
my head spins off
You find it in the closet
smelling your clothes

My day ricochets off fragile structures
Tin shed body
Tiny barking dog in my gut

The things we lock inside eat our tails
There aren't enough bells ringing
anymore

* * *

Pre-spring is an evil time

I don't mean a time to do evil
I mean the waiting

My skin belongs to a dog

Yesterday a righteous old-timer
yelled at me for using my cells
It's none of his business

Age the reverse trumpet

I run from loneliness but that's habit
My therapist is obsessed with disasters
She's throwing a Titanic party

I cut my life into the tiniest pieces
and then eat them

* * *

When the prompt is "lost"
no one has any trouble

I try not to think about
what my sink has seen
The other renters' foam

Still the day relieves itself
of itself

You are in a separate place
where nothing rhymes
I clunk my planet across it

I want to ask if you ever
imagine me in a field

More unlikely

a white horse

* * *

To forgive is
the most active verb

Delicious isn't it
the long walk home
while everything comes to life
in your face

Descent a tactile waste
Just feel all the flowers
their tongues are lapping

Imprecision is a thing now
haven't you noticed

My pallet expander got in the way
of everything I ever wanted

A trajectory of rabbits softer than you
can imagine are the only creatures
to find their way home

When a fox crosses the road
in front of your car
that doesn't mean bad luck

it just means watch out for foxes
We need more adages

Today I ruined a few things
separate from my intention

I hear that Mercury is in retrograde

I stayed up all night
worrying about falling asleep

Soon I'll be a message
on Winter's answering machine

* * *

Take your animal out
I am always hungry for something

Cougars aren't teaching their cubs
to be afraid anymore
So now what

Thank god for our bodies
and their engravings

What happened to you
pounds of dust and ash
We need to keep breathing
do the required survival

Everything else
a holster for our guns

* * *

I take it personally
when you fall asleep while I'm talking
I tail you into dreams

I want to scope your insides
and hang the photos

Thinner than an eggshell
the heart's membrane
dividing us from disaster

You swinging an axe

Take me outside
and split my hands into
a thousand pieces

then plant them back
in the ground

* * *

Weak senses make us scared
of the dark
Even daylight hunts

Have you heard a rabbit scream
You'll never recover

When I am far enough away
to make you indistinguishable
I start walking towards you again

We are teething on privacy
and the distance of a rubber band

Evil reminds me of being alone in a room

Last night I was both the bride
and the groom

Love goes off in the woods
and comes back with a bear
Don't ever discount this

A quick death is a mercy
A thousand times a thousand claws

For that split second
does our body miss us

before something else arrives

About the Author

Sarah Bartlett lives in Portland, OR. She is the author of two chapbooks, *My Only Living Relative*, published by Phantom Books in 2015, and *Freud Blah Blah Blah*, published by Rye House Press in 2014. She has also co-authored two chapbook collaborations. Her recent work has appeared or is forthcoming in: *Lit, Fruita Pulp, Cloudbanks & Shimbleshanks, The Volta, Sixth Finch, Alice Blue*, and elsewhere.

Acknowledgments

Freud Blah Blah Blah was published as a chapbook by *Rye House Press* in 2014

"I paint a wall in my bedroom blue" appeared in *Coconut*.

"When you take apart the small thing there is," "Pets are stupid. I've never understood why," "I want to drop a tiny white feather into you," "Suffering is having your body full of nails," "My mother dreamt she gave birth to a wolf," "Your purple t-shirt should have a horse on it," "Can I live vicariously through your ekphrasis?" appeared in *Spork*.

"Wood has it's own animal smell," "Inside the sweat machine we run our mouths," "I'll make you a wolverine fur coat so you can climb," "We go to a rock show and touch shoulders," "I will Evel Knievel you so hard until fish come out," "Last night I dreamt you were a Cat Stevens record," "When we go into the jungle, I'm tired of being the one," appeared in *Eleven Eleven* and were nominated for a 2013 Pushcart Prize.

Wintertime Makes Me Honest appeared in *Phantom Limb*

Strange Bravery I Pay The Gods For appeared in *Heavy Feather Review*

Immortality Is So Whimsical, Our Nuclear Payload is Fully Loaded appeared in *Sixth Finch*

St. Augustine's Lost Entry, Being Unhorsed Vs. Being Unsaddled appeared in *iO*

They Are Breathing All Around appeared in *Inter|rupture*

If I Could Only Find You, I'd Find You appeared in *New Delta Review*

Sections from Sometimes We Walk With Our Nails Out appeared *Swine*

Being From Here appeared in *Fruita Pulp*

I'd like to thank the editors of the journals in which these poems first appeared. So much gratitude goes out to my friends and family for their support and feedback, with a special shout to the following people who provided invaluable insight on this project: Emily Kendal Frey, Airin Miller, Dan Boehl, and Coleman Stevenson.

Subito Press Titles

2014

Liner Notes by James Brubaker

As We Know by Amaranth Borsuk & Andy Finch

Letters & Buildings by Thomas Hummel

2016

New Animals by Nick Francis Potter

Sometimes We Walk With Our Nails Out by Sarah Bartlett

To Think of Her Writing Awash in Light by Linda Russo

Someone Took They Tongues. by Douglas Kearney

About Subito Press

Subito Press is a non-profit literary publisher based in the Creative Writing Program of the Department of English at the University of Colorado at Boulder. Subito Press encourages and supports work that challenges already-accepted literary modes and devices.

Subito Press

Noah Eli Gordon, *director*
Liz McGehee, *managing editor*
Kolby Harvey
Sarah Thompson
Rebecca Kallemeyn
Oakley Chad Meredith
Eleanor Haberl
Scott Goodstein
Lance Duncan